Phonics

This book belongs to
....

Colour the star when you complete a page.
See how far you've come!

Author: Sasha Wigley

How to use this book

This book is designed to recap and consolidate your child's knowledge of phonics taught up to the end of Year 1. It follows the recommended phonics system and order used in most schools. Activities increase in difficulty as your child works through the book in order to stretch and challenge their subject knowledge.

- Find a quiet, comfortable place to work, away from distractions.
- This book has been written in a logical order, so start at the first page and work your way through.
- Help with reading the instructions where necessary and ensure that your child understands what to do.
- Encourage your child to sound out each letter sound before they attempt to blend the sounds together to read the word.
- Some sounds are represented by two letters. These are called digraphs. For example, sh and ch. For these sounds your child should sound out the single sh or ch sound and not the individual letter sounds.
- Always end each activity on a positive note and before your child gets tired so that they will be eager to return next time.
- Help and encourage your child to check their own answers as they complete each activity.
- Let your child return to their favourite pages once they have been completed. Talk about the activities they enjoyed and what they have learned.

Special features of this book:

- **Progress chart:** when your child has completed a page, ask them to colour in the relevant star on the first page of this book. This will enable you to keep track of progress through the activities and help to motivate your child.
- **Learning tip:** found throughout the book in a yellow box at the bottom of a page, these give you some suggested talking points based around the page topic.

Scan the QR code with your smartphone to access free audio content. Here you will find the correct pronunciation of sounds learned in this book.

Published by Collins
An imprint of HarperCollins*Publishers* Ltd
The News Building
1 London Bridge Street
London
SE1 9GF

HarperCollins*Publishers*
Macken House, 39/40 Mayor Street Upper, Dublin 1
D01 C9W8, Ireland

Browse the complete Collins catalogue at www.collins.co.uk

© HarperCollins*Publishers* Ltd 2023
First published 2023

10 9 8 7 6 5 4 3 2 1

ISBN 978-0-00-861792-9

The author asserts the moral right to be identified as the author of this work.

All rights reserved. No part of this publication may be reproduced, stored in a retrieval system, or transmitted, in any form or by any means, electronic, mechanical, photocopying, recording or otherwise, without the prior permission of Collins.

British Library Cataloguing in Publication Data.

A Catalogue record for this publication is available from the British Library.

Author: Sasha Wigley
Publisher: Jennifer Hall
Project management and editorial: Chantal Addy
Design and layout: Sarah Duxbury and Contentra Technologies Ltd
Cover: Amparo Barrera and Sarah Duxbury
All images: ©Shutterstock.com and ©HarperCollins*Publishers*
Production: Emma Wood
Printed in Great Britain by Martins the Printers

Contents

Simple sounds	4
Vowel digraphs and trigraphs	6
More complex words	8
Adjacent consonants	9
Tricky words 1	10
ay, ea, ou and oy sounds	11
ie, ir and ue sounds	12
aw, ew and ie sounds	13
ey, ph and wh sounds	14
Split digraphs i–e and o–e	15
Split digraphs a–e, e–e and u–e	16
Letters a, e, i, o and u	17
Other ways to spell s, v and z	18
Other ways to spell oa and oo	19
Other ways to spell e, l and u	20
Letters ch and y	21
Other ways to spell ur	22
What is a schwa?	23
Other ways to spell air and ear	24
When a sounds like o	25
Silent letters	26
Other ways to spell j, sh and zh	27
Other ways to spell ai	28
Other ways to spell or	29
Tricky words 2	30
Answers	31

Simple sounds

The first sounds you learn on your phonics journey are those on the sound wall below. Once you know these sounds, you can blend them together to read words.

1 Say each sound on the sound wall. Colour the sounds that you sound out correctly.

	s	a	t	p	i	n	m
d	g	o	c	k	ck	e	u
	r	h	b	f	l	ff	ll
ss	j	v	w	x	y	z	
	zz	qu	ch	sh	th	ng	nk

2 Read the words. Draw a line to match each word to the correct picture.

red sock

big hill

pink wig

quick fox

hot chips

3 Read the words on each domino. (Circle) the word that matches the picture.

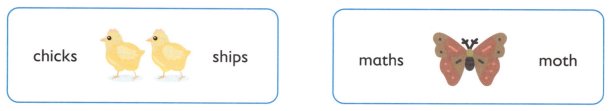

chicks   ships

maths   moth

4 Sound out the sounds on the jigsaw pieces. Blend them together to make a word.

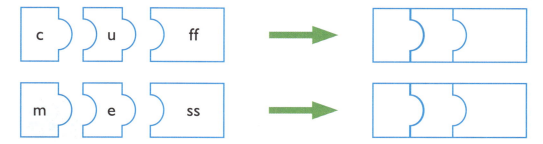

c   u   ff   →

m   e   ss   →

5 Say what you see in each picture. Sound out the word slowly. Write the word in the word frame. The first one has been done for you.

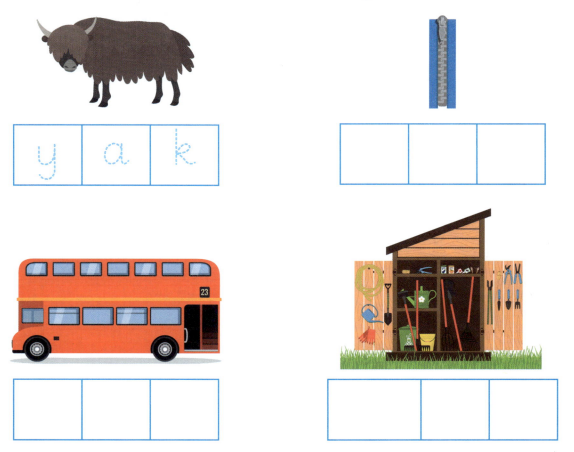

y a k

Try to pronounce each sound clearly. It is important not to add an 'uh' sound when sounding out letters. For example, it is 'mmm' not 'muh' and 'b' not 'buh'.

Vowel digraphs and trigraphs

A digraph is one sound formed with two letters. For example, **ai** as in r**ai**n.
A trigraph is one sound formed with three letters. For example, **ear** as in d**ear**.

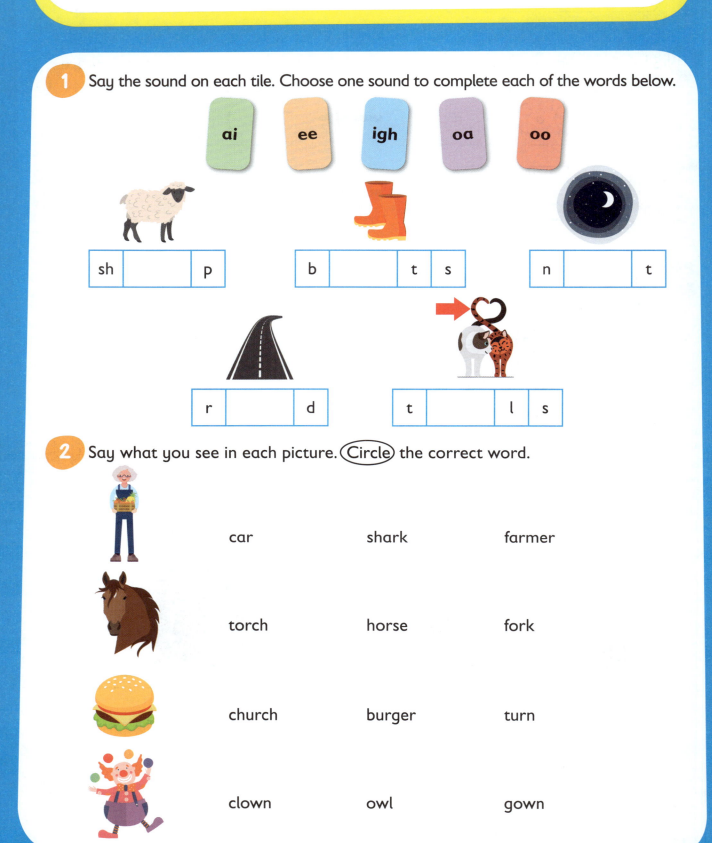

3) Read the words in the box. Choose the correct word to write below each picture.

| fair   beard   tear   hair   stairs   ear |

_____   _____   _____

_____   _____   _____

4) Read each sentence below. Complete the smiley face after you have read each sentence.

I go to sleep in the rain.

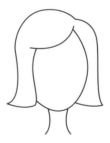

'Are you sure?' he said.

Her hair was short.

More complex words

Once you have learned the simple sounds, you will be able to start reading longer words with double letters and common endings such as **–ing** and **–ed**. You will also be able to decode some compound words. These are words created by joining two shorter words together. For example, arm + chair = armchair.

1 Read each word carefully. Draw a line to match the word to the correct picture.

| chatting | hugging | swimming | running | hopping |

2 Read the two words in each sum. Add them together and write the compound word under the correct picture. The first one has been done for you.

| tooth + brush | star + fish | rain + coat | post + box |

toothbrush _____ _____ _____

Play Verb Charades! Practise orally adding the –ing and –ed suffixes by miming action words (verbs) with your child. For example, **watching** or **clapping**. You can act out what you did yesterday to practise the past tense. For example, **watched** or **clapped**.

Adjacent consonants

Adjacent consonants are two or more consonants that appear next to each other in a word. For example, **s** and **t** in **stop**. Each consonant should be sounded out then blended together to read.

1. Say the sounds on the tiles. Choose one to complete the word frames below. Now read the words and listen out for the adjacent consonants.

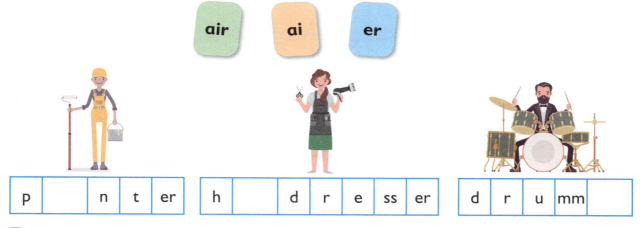

| p | | n | t | er |

| h | | d | r | e | ss | er |

| d | r | u | mm | |

2. Read the words. Colour the matching picture in the correct colour.

the biggest red   the highest green   the strongest orange

3. Read each sentence. Underline the sentence which matches the picture.

Ben clapped his hands.

I looked into my lunchbox.

She was sleeping in a bunkbed.

Blending adjacent consonants can be tricky at first. Be patient, point examples out when reading with your child and sound them out clearly.

Tricky words 1

Tricky words cannot easily be decoded or sounded out using the sounds that you have learned so far. It is important that you learn to read these words as they appear a lot in your reading books. Tricky words are practised throughout this book to help you get to know them.

1 Say the tricky word on each star. Colour the star if you can read the word.

is	I	the	as	and	has	his
her	go	no	to	into	she	he
we	be	me	of	was	you	they
my	by	all	are	so	said	have
like	some	come	love	do	were	here
little	says	there	when	what	one	out	today

2 Choose one of the tricky words above. Write a sentence using this word.

_____

_____

Create colourful tricky word flashcards together to use in games such as Snap or Pairs. It is also fun to spot tricky words in the books you read together or on signs when you are out and about.

ay, ea, ou and oy sounds

There is often more than one way to spell the same sound. For example, the **ai** sound in r**ai**n and d**ay**. Trace the digraph in the words below. Read each word.

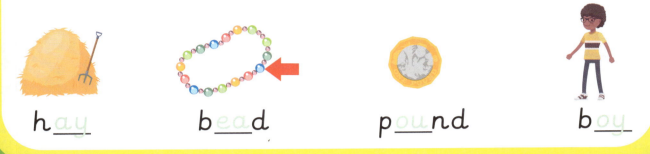

h__ay__   b__ea__d   p__ou__nd   b__oy__

1 Say the sounds on the tiles. Choose the correct digraph to complete each word.

ay   ou   oy   ea

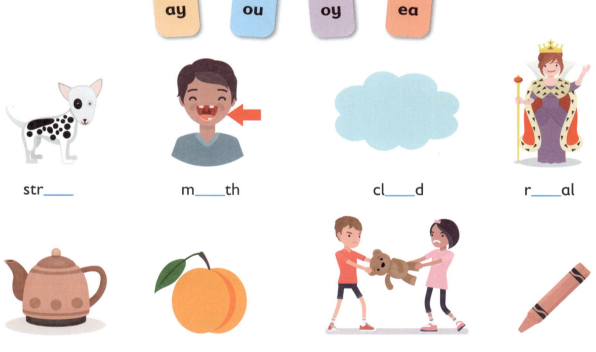

str____   m____th   cl____d   r____al

t____pot   p____ch   ann____   cr____on

2 Read each sentence. (Circle) the sentence that matches the picture.

On Sunday, we are going to the football ground.

I enjoy playing with my cowboy toy.

The teacher reads about the stingray.

11

ie, ir and ue sounds

Trace the digraph in the words below. Read each word.

t_ie_   sk_ir_t   stat_ue_

1 Say what you see in each picture. Circle the sound that you can hear in the word.

| oy | ir | | ay | ie | | ue | ou |

| ea | ue | | ie | ee | | ir | ai |

2 Read each sentence. Circle the correct word to complete the sentence.

The [girl / gurl] comes [ferst / first] in the running race.

We [trighd / tried] to eat the [fries / frighs].

On [Toosday / Tuesday], I will put on my [blue / bloo] shirt.

aw, ew and ie sounds

Trace the digraph in the words below. Read each word.

l_aw_n   scr_ew_   sh_ie_ld

1 Say what you see in each picture. Circle the correct word.

news   jewel   chew

crawl   seesaw   jigsaw

field   smoothie   thief

2 Read each sentence. Tick the sentence that matches the picture.

I can draw an owl with claws. ☐

They grew a few new flowers. ☐

Play sorting games to group together words containing the same sound. Start by grouping words with the same initial sound, for example **book, box, bunny** and then those with the same final sound, for example **car, star, jar**. Sounds that appear in the middle of words can be hardest to hear. Once they are confident enough, challenge your child to group these together too, for example **bird, thirsty, curl**.

ey, ph and wh sounds

Trace the digraph in the words below. Read each word.

troll_ey_   _ph_one   _wh_isk

1 Read each word. Draw a line to match the word to the correct picture.

| whiskers | alphabet | donkey | wheel | key | dolphin |

2 Read the words in the box. Choose the correct word to write below each picture.

| elephant | chimney | whisper |

_____   _____   _____

3 Read each sentence. Find and underline the digraph given on the tile.

wh — Whitney whirls in her wheelchair.

ph — Philip the phantom likes phonics.

ey — Jeffrey the jockey gallops in the valley.

Split digraphs i-e and o-e

A split digraph consists of two vowels which are split by a consonant. For example, **pine**, **game**, **June**. The split vowels together make the long vowel sound.

p i n e   g a m e   J u n e

1 Say what you see in each picture. Choose the correct split digraph to complete the word.

sm__l__

c__n__

h__m__

pr__z__

envel__p__

outs__d__

2 Read each sentence. Spot the split digraphs. The first one has been found for you.

My wife likes to drive in the sunshine.

The tadpole had a home under a stone.

Mr Pine has a phone and a telescope.

Go on a split digraph word hunt. Use a curved pipe cleaner to link the two letters in the split digraph. This will help your child to quickly recognise split digraphs when they are reading.

15

Split digraphs a-e, e-e and u-e

1 Read each word. Draw a line to match the word to the correct picture.

| whale | evening | cube |

2 Say what you see in each picture. Complete the words by writing the missing split digraph in the word frame.

a–e   e–e   u–e

c__t__   panc__k__s   trap__z__

3 Complete each sentence using the words from the boxes. Read the sentences.

_____ m**a**de a _____ . | K**a**te | mist**a**ke |

_____ and P**e**te _____ in a r**a**ce. | comp**e**te | St**e**ve |

J**u**ne plays a _____ on her _____ . | fl**u**te | t**u**ne |

16

Letters a, e, i, o and u

The vowels **a**, **e**, **i**, **o**, and **u** can make a short or long sound. Say each pair of words below and listen to the different sound that the vowel makes in each.

| can acorn | bun music | pen evil |
| kid child | dog oval | |

1 Read each clue. Choose the correct answer from the box.

| bagel   hello   unicorn   equals   silent |

You might say this when you greet someone.   _____

In maths, what does = mean?   _____

An animal with one long horn.   _____

Something you might eat for breakfast.   _____

No sound at all.   _____

2 Say what you see in each picture. Complete the word with the correct vowel. Read each word.

__ngel   volcan__   k__nd   men__   s__cret

Other ways to spell s, v and z

The graphemes **st**, **se**, **ce** and **c** can make the sound **s**.

The sound **v** can be represented with the grapheme **ve**. This is usually used at the end of a word.

The graphemes **ze** and **se** can sound like **z**.

1 Read each word. <u>Underline</u> the grapheme shown on the tile in each word.

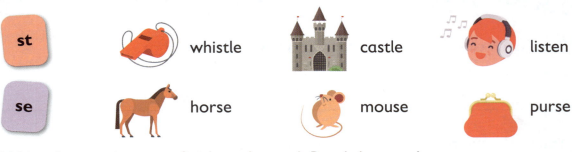

| st | whistle | castle | listen |
| se | horse | mouse | purse |

Write the grapheme to finish each word. Read the word.

| ce | fen____ | dan____ | prin____ |
| c | ____ity | fa__e | i__y |

2 Read each word. Draw a line to match the word to the correct picture.

| give | twelve | love | active |

3 Read each sentence. Draw a line to match the sentence to the correct picture.

Please can I have some cheese?

I will sneeze if you squeeze me.

Other ways to spell oa and oo

The phonic sound **oa** can be spelt with the graphemes **oe**, **ow** or **ou**.

The phonic sound **oo** can be spelt with the graphemes **ui** or **ou**. Remember **oo** can be long as in gl**oo**m or short as in l**oo**k.

1 Add the grapheme **oe** to each of the words below. Read the word.

domin____s   tipt____   potat____s

2 Add the grapheme **ou** to each of the words below. Read the word.

sh____lder   b____lder   m____ld

3 Read the words below. Write the correct word under each picture.

| rainbow | pillow | throw | shadow |

_____   _____   _____   _____

4 Look at each picture. Circle the word that fits the picture best.

cruise   bruise   fruit   juice   swimsuit   suitcase

5 Read each sentence. <u>Underline</u> the long **oo** sounds in blue and the short **oo** in red. The first two examples have been done for you.

You should join the youth group.

Would you like soup?

19

Other ways to spell e, l and u

The phonic sound **l** at the end of a word can be spelt with the graphemes **le** or **al**. Sometimes the sound **e** is spelt with the grapheme **ea**.

1 Use the sounds on the tiles to build the word shown by each picture.

bb	u	b	le	_____
le	u	p	zz	_____
m	le	ar	b	_____

2 Read the words in the box. Complete each sentence using one of the words.

| hospital | metal | animals |

Robots are made of _____.

My friend was sick and had to go to _____.

Mice are my favourite _____.

3 Read the words. Draw a line to match the rhyming words.

| head | | weather |

| feather | | bread |

4 Read each sentence. Notice how the grapheme on the star sounds in each sentence. <u>Underline</u> the words that include the sound on the star.

☆ o Last Monday, my brother won a monkey!

☆ ou A couple of young girls got into trouble.

☆ o–e I would love to wear some gloves.

Letters ch and y

The grapheme **ch** can be pronounced in a few different ways. For example, e**ch**o and **ch**ef.

The grapheme **y** can be pronounced in a few different ways. For example, happ**y**, fl**y** and g**y**m.

1 Read the words in the box. Notice how the grapheme **ch** sounds in each word. Write the word below the correct picture.

| Christmas anchor machine school parachute |

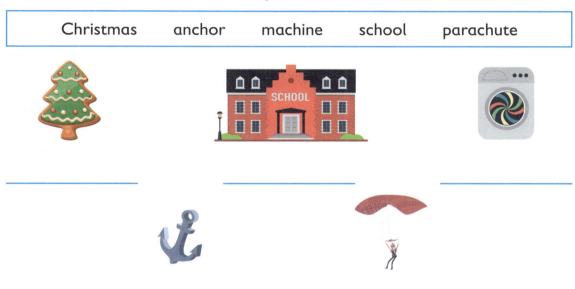

2 Read the words on each domino. Circle the word that matches the picture.

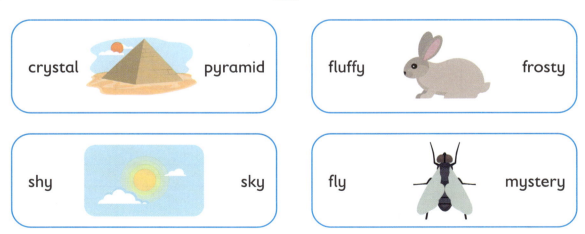

When you come across a grapheme that can be pronounced in different ways, encourage your child to sound out all the pronunciations they have learned. Discuss which one sounds right and give lots of praise for their efforts! It will become easier with practice.

Other ways to spell ur

The phonic sound **ur** can be spelt with the graphemes **ear** and **or**.

1 Read the words. Colour the pictures.

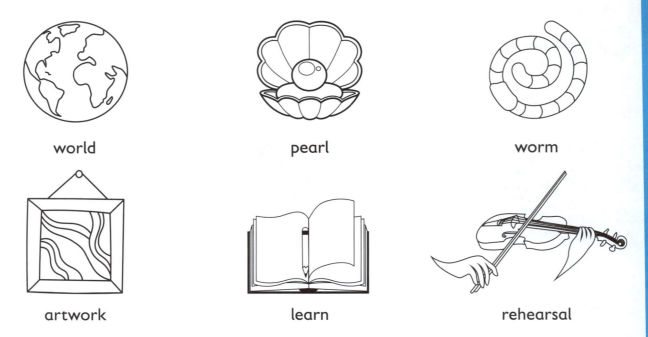

world   pearl   worm

artwork   learn   rehearsal

2 Blend the sounds on the jigsaw pieces together to make a word.

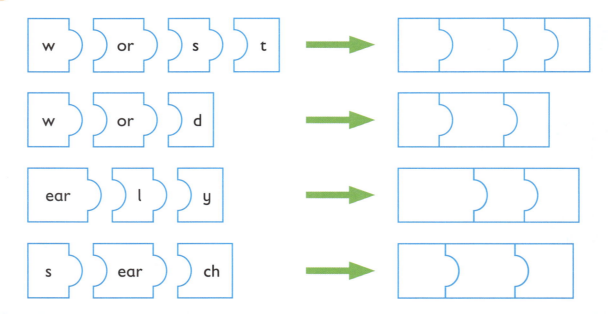

Try to keep on top of which sounds your child is learning at school and get creative at home. Create word art using paint, stickers, feathers, pasta, dough, glitter – the list goes on!

What is a schwa?

A lot of words contain a short **er** sound. This sound is called a schwa. A schwa sound can be represented by many different graphemes. Read the words below and notice the same short **er** sound made by the highlighted grapheme.

doct**or**   hamm**er**   probl**e**m   **a**gain

1 Read each word. Draw a line to match the word to the picture.

| Keny**a** | col**our** | togeth**er** | calend**ar** | mirr**or** |

2 Read the words in the box. Can you hear the schwa sound in each? Choose the correct word to write below each picture.

| octopus   thousand   wizard   different   pencil |

_____   _____   _____

_____   _____

Other ways to spell air and ear

> The sound **air** can be spelt with the graphemes **are**, **ear** or **ere**.
>
> The sound **ear** can be spelt with the graphemes **eer** or **ere**.

1 Say what you see in each picture. Add the correct trigraph from the stars to the word frames. The first one has been done for you.

☆ air   ☆ ear   ☆ are   ☆ ere

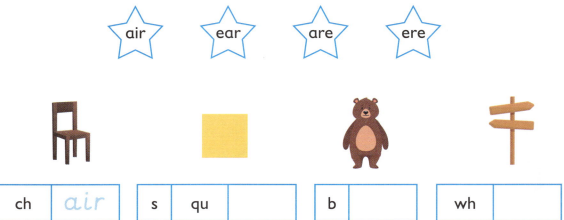

| ch | *air* | | s | qu | | | b | | | wh | |

2 Read each sentence. Underline the trigraph that makes the **ear** sound. Draw a line to match the sentence to the correct picture.

Here is a sphere.

The meerkats are cheerful.

3 Homophones are words that sound the same but have different meanings. Draw a line to match the picture to the correct word in each box.

When a sounds like o

Sometimes the grapheme **a** is pronounced **o**. Usually this happens when the grapheme **a** follows the grapheme **w**. This sounds complicated but there are a lot of common words with this pattern. For example, w**a**nt.

1 Read each word. Draw a line to match the word to the correct picture.

| watch | swan | wasp | wand | squash |

2 Read each word. Trace the word. Without looking, write the word in the final box.

Read	Trace	Write (no peeking)
want	*want*	
what	*what*	
was	*was*	

Help your child to practise their spellings each week by using the Read, Trace, Write table above. This is a great way for them to familiarise themselves with spelling patterns as well as tricky words.

Silent letters

Some letters can appear in a word but not make a sound. The letters **b**, **g**, **k** and **w** are silent when they appear in the following pairs: **mb**, **gn**, **kn**, **wr**.

1 Read the word. Notice which letter is silent.

knight   lamb   gnat   wren

2 Read the words on each domino. Circle the word that matches the picture.

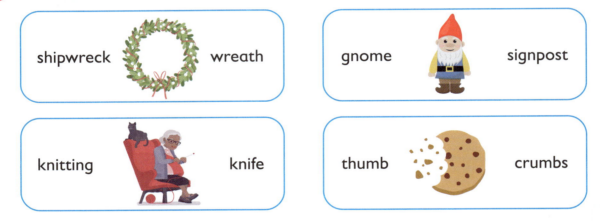

shipwreck — wreath

gnome — signpost

knitting — knife

thumb — crumbs

3 Read each sentence. Circle the correct word to complete the sentence.

Her [wrist / rist] was too sore to [right / write].

I [new / knew] it was [wrong / rong] to unwrap the present.

Can you [coam / comb] the [knots / nots] out of my hair?

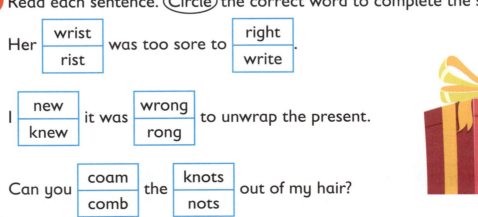

26

Other ways to spell j, sh and zh

The sound **j** can be spelt with the graphemes **g**, **ge** or **dge**.

The sound **sh** can be spelt with the graphemes **ci**, **si**, **ssi** or **ti**.

Sometimes the graphemes **su** and **si** make the sound **zh**. Say the words below and listen for the sound **zh**.

u**su**al   colli**si**on

1 Read the words in the box. Write the correct word under each picture.

| ma**g**ic | **g**iant | ba**dge**r | bri**dge** | lar**ge** | frin**ge** |

_____   _____   _____   _____   _____   _____

2 Read the words in the box. Write the correct word under each picture.

| po**ti**on | man**si**on | magi**ci**an | pa**ssi**onfruit |

_____   _____   _____   _____

3 Read each word. Draw a line to match each picture to the correct word. Colour in the pictures.

| televi**si**on | trea**su**re | explo**si**on | mea**su**re |

Other ways to spell ai

You already know some ways to spell the phonic sound **ai**: **ai, ay, a–e, a**. Here are some other ways:

eight   straight   they   break

1 Read each phrase. Listen for the sound 'ai' in the words. Draw a line to match the phrase to the correct picture.

- a grey train
- a straight rake
- a painted sleigh
- eighteen cupcakes
- a great steak

2 Colour the balls the correct colour.

eigh =   aigh =   ey =   ea =

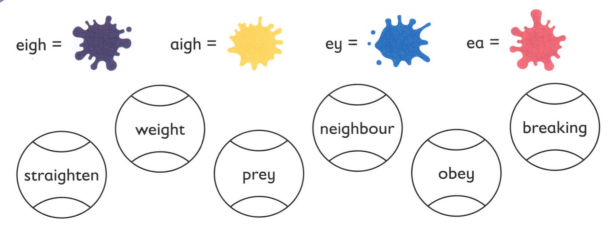

straighten, weight, prey, neighbour, obey, breaking

When spelling, it can be very difficult to decide which grapheme to choose for some sounds, for example the sound **ai** above. Encourage your child to try different options and to go with the one that looks right or familiar.

Other ways to spell or

You already know some ways to spell the phonic sound **or**: **or, au, aw**. Here are some other ways:

c**augh**t   p**our**   **oar**   m**ore**   w**al**k   th**ough**t

1 Read each phrase. Listen for the sound **or** in the words. Draw a line to match the phrase to the correct picture.

| the roaring lion |

| my daughter's ball |

| pour more tea |

| four apple cores |

| explore over the wall |

2 Read each sentence. Listen for the sound **or**. Colour the grapheme tiles that are in the sentence.

I caught the ball before it soared away. | al | ore | oar | augh |

You talked so much your throat will be sore. | our | ore | aw | al |

He thought he bought a skateboard. | ough | oar | our | ore |

When reading with your child, point out how sentences begin with a capital letter and end with a full stop. This will help them to remember punctuation when writing their own sentences.

Tricky words 2

1 Say the tricky word on each of the crayons. Colour the crayon if you can read the word.

- their
- people
- oh
- your
- Mr
- Mrs
- Ms
- could
- would
- should
- our
- house
- mouse
- water
- want
- any
- many
- again
- who
- whole
- where
- two
- school
- call
- different
- thought
- through
- friend
- work
- once
- laugh
- because
- eye
- busy
- beautiful
- pretty
- hour
- move
- improve
- ask
- parents
- shoe

2 Point to a crayon. Think of a sentence that uses this tricky word. Repeat with another tricky word. Write one of your sentences below.

_____

_____

Answers

Page 4
1. Child to pronounce sounds accurately.
2. Child to draw a line to match the word to the appropriate picture.

Page 5
3. chicks, moth
4. c–u–ff, m–e–ss
5. yak, zip, bus, shed

Page 6
1. sh**ee**p, b**oo**ts, n**igh**t, r**oa**d, t**ai**ls
2. farmer, horse, burger, clown

Page 7
3. hair, beard, fair, ear, stairs, tear
4. Child to read each sentence accurately and draw smiley faces.

Page 8
1. Child to draw a line to match the word to the appropriate picture.
2. raincoat, postbox, starfish

Page 9
1. p**ai**nter, h**ai**rdresser, drumm**er**
2. red lollipop, green mountain, orange weightlifter
3. I looked into my lunchbox.

Page 10
1. Child to pronounce words accurately.
2. Child to write accurate sentence.

Page 11
1. str**ay**, m**ou**th, cl**ou**d, r**oy**al, tea**po**t, p**ea**ch, ann**oy**, cr**ay**on
2. (The teacher reads about the stingray)

Page 12
1. b**ir**d, p**ie**, gl**ue**, bl**ue**, fr**ie**d egg, th**ir**teen
2. girl first, tried fries, Tuesday blue

Page 13
1. jewel, jigsaw, smoothie
2. They grew a few new flowers. ✔

Page 14
1. Child to draw a line to match the word to the appropriate picture.
2. chimney, whisper, elephant
3. **Wh**itney **wh**irls **wh**eelchair
   Philip **ph**antom **ph**onics
   Jeffr**ey** jock**ey** vall**ey**

Page 15
1. smil**e**, c**o**ne, h**o**me, pri**ze**, envel**o**pe, outsi**de**
2. w**i**fe, l**i**kes, dr**i**ve, sunsh**i**ne tadp**o**le, h**o**me, st**o**ne P**i**ne, ph**o**ne, telesc**o**pe

Page 16
1. Child to draw a line to match the word to the appropriate picture.
2. c**u**te, panc**a**kes, trap**eze**
3. Kate made a mistake. Steve and Pete compete in a race.
   June plays a tune on her flute.

Page 17
1. hello, equals, unicorn, bagel, silent
2. **a**ngel, volcan**o**, k**i**nd, men**u**, s**e**cret

Page 18
1. Child to pronounce words accurately.
   whi**stle**, ca**stle**, li**sten**
   hor**se**, mou**se**, pur**se**
   fen**ce**, dan**ce**, prin**ce**
   city, fa**ce**, **i**cy
2. Child to draw a line to match the word to the appropriate picture.
3. Child to draw a line to match the sentence to the appropriate picture.

Page 19
1. domino**es**, tipt**oe**, potat**oes**
2. sh**ou**lder, b**ou**lder, m**ou**ld
3. pillow, throw, rainbow, shadow
4. cruise, fruit, suitcase
5. Y**ou**, sh**ou**ld, y**ou**th, gr**ou**p W**ou**ld, y**ou**, s**ou**p

Page 20
1. bubble, puzzle, marble
2. metal, hospital, animals
3. head – bread, feather – weather
4. M<u>o</u>nday, br<u>o</u>ther, w<u>o</u>n, m<u>o</u>nkey, c<u>ou</u>ple, y<u>ou</u>ng, tr<u>ou</u>ble l<u>o</u>ve, s<u>o</u>me, gl<u>o</u>ves

Page 21
1. Christmas, school, machine, anchor, parachute
2. pyramid, fluffy, sky, fly

Page 22
1. Child to pronounce words accurately and colour the pictures.
2. worst, word, early, search

Page 23
1. Child to draw a line to match the word to the appropriate picture.
2. wizard, octopus, different, pencil, thousand

Page 24
1. ch<u>air</u>, squ<u>are</u>, b<u>ear</u>, wh<u>ere</u>
2. h<u>ere</u>, sph<u>ere</u> m<u>ee</u>rkats, ch<u>ee</u>rful
   Child to draw a line to match each sentence to the correct picture.
3. Child to draw a line to match the word to the appropriate picture.

Page 25
1. Child to draw a line to match the word to the appropriate picture.
2. Child to spell each word accurately.

Page 26
1. Child to pronounce each word accurately. Silent letters: k, b, g, w
2. wreath, gnome, knitting, crumbs
3. wrist, write knew, wrong comb, knots

Page 27
1. badger, magic, fringe, giant, large, bridge
2. passionfruit, potion, magician, mansion
3. Child to draw a line to match the word to an appropriate picture.

Page 28
1. Child to draw a line to match the phrase to the appropriate picture.
2. weight, neighbour
   straighten
   prey, obey
   breaking

Page 29
1. Child to draw a line to match the phrase to the appropriate picture.
2. augh, al, ore, oar
   al, our, ore
   ough, oar

Page 30
1. Child to pronounce words accurately.
2. Child to write sentence accurately.